797,885 Books
are available to read at

Forgotten Books

www.ForgottenBooks.com

Forgotten Books' App
Available for mobile, tablet & eReader

ISBN 978-1-331-20185-4
PIBN 10157732

This book is a reproduction of an important historical work. Forgotten Books uses state-of-the-art technology to digitally reconstruct the work, preserving the original format whilst repairing imperfections present in the aged copy. In rare cases, an imperfection in the original, such as a blemish or missing page, may be replicated in our edition. We do, however, repair the vast majority of imperfections successfully; any imperfections that remain are intentionally left to preserve the state of such historical works.

Forgotten Books is a registered trademark of FB &c Ltd.
Copyright © 2015 FB &c Ltd.
FB &c Ltd, Dalton House, 60 Windsor Avenue, London, SW19 2RR.
Company number 08720141. Registered in England and Wales.

For support please visit www.forgottenbooks.com

1 MONTH OF FREE READING

at

www.ForgottenBooks.com

By purchasing this book you are eligible for one month membership to ForgottenBooks.com, giving you unlimited access to our entire collection of over 700,000 titles via our web site and mobile apps.

To claim your free month visit:

www.forgottenbooks.com/free157732

* Offer is valid for 45 days from date of purchase. Terms and conditions apply.

Similar Books Are Available from
www.forgottenbooks.com

The Christian Mythology
by Brigham Leatherbee

Jesus and What He Said
by Arthur Salter Burrows

Reincarnation in the New Testament
by James Morgan Pryse

Dictionary of the Holy Bible
by William Wilberforce Rand

Being a Christian
by Jas A. Duncan

Heaven
by Dwight Lyman Moody

How to Pray
by R. A. Torrey

The Bible and Evolution
by W. H. Sparshott

The Aquarian Gospel of Jesus the Christ
by Levi

Christ and His Church in the Book of Psalms
by Andrew A. Bonar

Christian Healing
A Sermon Delivered at Boston, by Mary Baker Eddy

Church History Through All Ages
by Thomas Timpson

The Life of Jesus, Vol. 1 of 2
For the People, by David Friedrich Strauss

The Serpent, Satan and False Prophet
Or the Trinity of Evil, by Unknown Author

The Christian Faith and the Old Testament
by John M. Thomas

Christianity and Sex Problems
by Hugh Northcote

The Evolution of Spiritual Man
by William McIntire Lisle

The Beacon of Truth
Or Testimony of the Coran to the Truth of the Christian Religion, by William Muir

A Biblical View of the Church
by Josiah Goodman Bishop

Muhammad and Christ
by Moulvi Muhammad Ali

A POPULAR ACCOUNT
OF THE
NEWLY-RECOVERED
GOSPEL OF ST. PETER

THE NEWLY-RECOVERED APOLOGY OF ARISTIDES

Its Doctrine and Ethics; with Selected Passages from Professor J. Rendel Harris' Translation.

By HELEN B. HARRIS.

Second Edition.

Handsomely bound. Crown 8vo, 2s. 6d. With frontispiece.

"Exceedingly interesting."—*Athenæum*.

"It should be put into every Christian library, that it may be read by young and old. No more beautiful or useful present can be made to a young minister, or indeed to any one else. We would have it scattered far and wide in all Churches, and among working men by thousands."—*Methodist Recorder*.

London:
HODDER & STOUGHTON, 27, Paternoster Row.

A POPULAR ACCOUNT

OF THE

NEWLY-RECOVERED
GOSPEL OF ST. PETER

BY

J. RENDEL HARRIS

FELLOW OF CLARE COLLEGE, CAMBRIDGE

London

HODDER AND STOUGHTON

27 PATERNOSTER ROW

MDCCCXCIII.

Printed by Hazell, Watson, & Viney, Ld., London and Aylesbury.

PREFACE.

IN the following pages I have tried to give an account of the most recent discovery in theological literature, the Gospel attributed to St. Peter, in such a form as to familiarise the mind of the non-technical reader with some of the results which are being arrived at by Biblical scholars, and which ought to be as encouraging to our faith as they are stimulating to the understanding. The Gospel of Peter, even in the imperfect form in which it has come down to us, is the breaking of a new seal, the opening of a fresh door, to those who are engaged in the problems presented by Biblical and Patristic criticism. We may expect anything, in the world of Christian letters, after such an astonishing discovery; if we do not realise our expectations, it will certainly be because, either at home or abroad, in labours philological or archæological, we are wicked and slothful servants.

CONTENTS.

CHAPTER I.
OF MODERN BIBLICAL AND PATRISTIC DISCOVERIES   3

CHAPTER II.
OF THE NEWLY-DISCOVERED DOCUMENTS FROM AKHMÎM 15

CHAPTER III.
THE DOCETIC GOSPEL OF PETER 25

CHAPTER IV.
THE EXTANT TEXT OF THE NEW GOSPEL . . 41

CHAPTER V.
ON THE SOURCES OF THE NEW GOSPEL . . 59

CHAPTER VI.

SOME UNCANONICAL PARALLELS TO THE GOSPEL OF PETER 75

CHAPTER VII.

CONCLUDING REMARKS 93

I.

OF MODERN BIBLICAL AND PATRISTIC DISCOVERIES.

CHAPTER I.

OF MODERN BIBLICAL AND PATRISTIC DIS-
COVERIES.

SOME days since, as I was examining a list of Patristic authorities which a modern scholar had indicated as necessary ground to be worked over in search of non-canonical parallels to the Christian Gospels, my attention was caught by the large proportion of the material cited which had become known within the last few years; for while there were a number of authorities referred to whose contents have been known from very early times, it would be no exaggeration to say that more than half of the books in question had seen the light, either wholly or in part, within the last five-and-twenty years; and their completeness or their first publication was due to earnest and painstaking work carried on in the great libraries of the East and West, or to the happy intuitions of some explorer or archæologist.

Many of these discoveries are well known to the world at large. Every one, for example, remembers the thrill of excitement which went through all Christian Churches when it was learned that a copy of the "Teaching of the Apostles," the earliest known book of Christian discipline, had been found in a library at Constantinople. How it was applauded and criticised, and endorsed and contradicted! What inquiry was made into its ethics, liturgics, and eschatology, and into the dogmatic statements which underlay them ! There are few Christian people who do not occupy themselves to some extent with the study of the origins of Christianity; and a new work which had to do with so important a subject—which belonged, perhaps, to the very century in which the faith was crystallised—was certain to attract an almost universal attention.

I was living in America at the time when Bishop Bryennios' great discovery saw the light, and can recall how the new tract was sold on the streets and conned in the railway cars, the meetings that were held in the churches for its more public reading, and the discussions to which it gave rise in newspapers and journals of every shade of opinion. It was the best evidence I had ever obtained of the hold of Christianity on the mind of the people, that they should be so fluttered by the publication of less than a dozen pages of an ancient Christian book from an Eastern library.

But it does not follow that the "Teaching of the Apostles" is the most important discovery of the period of which we are speaking. It had the advantage of completeness and of brevity, and it was, in spite of some obscurities, generally intelligible. But there have been many other discoveries of works almost contemporary with the "Teaching," which have not been capable of presentation in the simple straightforwardness which characterises a translation of its text. The stir which they have made has been in a narrower circle, but it has gone deeper. They have not been laid on the reading-desk in the church, but they have been read over and over in the study and in the lecture-room. Their message has been for the twentieth century rather than the nineteenth. To take an illustration, we may regard the discovery of Tatian's "Fourfold Gospel," or "Diatessaron," as vastly surpassing in importance the "Teaching of the Apostles": true, it has only come down to us in a time-worn form through translations, yet it has told us in unmistakable language of the place which the Gospel of John had acquired in the estimation of the Church by the middle of the second century, and rendered it easy to believe that the Fourth Gospel is substantially, what it pretends to be, a message not from an anonymous *attaché* of the philosophy current in Alexandria, but from the man that leaned on Jesus' breast, and, as St. Bernard says, drew from the heart of the Only-begotten what He had imbibed from the Father. But there are few people, as yet, who realise how revolutionary this discovery has been in the question of the genuineness and authenticity of the New Testament records, and how many idle criticisms it has silenced; the Gospel of John to-day stands the firmest of the four, and I have been in the habit of telling my students that, in consequence of the attention which has been bestowed upon it, its verified age —*i.e.*, the latest possible date to which it can be referred—goes back a year for every year that it is under examination. For my part, I think it is matter of thankfulness that some of these questions are being definitely settled, and that conclusions are being reached from which there will be no appeal; but I do not see how they could have been reached in a satisfactory manner except by the recovery of new materials, which is the last thing that some critics give their mind to.

Now, if past experience may be taken as a guide to our expectations, we should certainly be justified in saying that the next ten years ought to be very fruitful in new documents belonging to the first three centuries. If the lost Apology of Aristides on behalf of the Christian faith has been recovered, then certainly we ought to indulge the hope that the companion Apology of Quadratus is lurking somewhere. The only wonder is that it was not found in the very same volume of tracts on Mount Sinai which contained the Aristides : if Tatian's conglomerate gospel has been found, we ought not to despair of finding Papias and his book of explanations of the text of Mark ; and, further, there are great text-books of early heresies which once had so wide a circulation that it is hard to believe that they have wholly disappeared. What a light would be thrown upon the ecclesiastical life of the second century if we could find the book of "Contradictions" in which Marcion, the great heretic of the second century, "the wolf from Pontus," as he was called, contrasted the God of the Old Testament with the Father of the New Testament, and demonstrated, as he supposed, such an opposition between them that he almost became himself the founder of a new faith. Many of these missing books will yet turn up, and the heretical volumes will be even more interesting than those which belong properly to Catholic Theology; for at present we owe our knowledge of the primitive sects, which broke from or clustered round

Christianity, almost entirely to the statements which were made of them by the Doctors and Fathers of the Church.

A little reflection will also show that new documents may be expected to turn up in any part of the world. The "Teaching" was found in Constantinople, the Arabic version of Tatian partly in Rome and partly in Egypt; the Apology of Aristides lay on Mount Sinai, and the lost Refutation of Heresies by Hippolytus came from a monastery on Mount Athos; Ephrem's commentary or Tatian's Gospel came, if I remember rightly, partly from the Armenian convent at Venice, and partly from the similar institution at the foot of Mount Ararat. But it is to Egypt that we must more especially look in the coming days, for in the ruins of her cities and amongst her tombs there must yet lie a wealth of buried treasure in literature, which would make the world astonished. Especially should search be made and excavations carried on amongst the remains of cities belonging to the Christian era; for these, although not furnishing material to the student of Egyptology, are likely to contain many Christian and Greek documents. And, in fact, it is from Egypt that this last great· treasure-trove has come, which we are now to describe, as simply as possible, to our readers.

II.

OF THE NEWLY-DISCOVERED DOCUMENTS FROM AKHMÎM.

CHAPTER II.

OF THE NEWLY-DISCOVERED DOCUMENTS FROM AKHMÎM.

A VOLUME has recently been published at Paris containing the results of the investigations of the French Archæological Mission at Cairo.* It is the ninth volume of a series of studies in Egyptology and associated matters; but the volume in question is wholly made of Greek documents which have been found by excavation amongst the Christian

---

* Is there any English Archæological Mission in Egypt? and if not, why not?

tombs in Akhmîm, in Upper Egypt. The major part of the book is concerned with the decipherment and interpretation of a papyrus containing a discussion in Greek arithmetic. But at the end of the book there will be found the contents of a vellum MS. of thirty-three leaves, containing portions of no less than three lost Christian works—viz., the Book of Enoch, the Gospel of Peter, and the Apocalypse of Peter. The size of the pages is about six inches by four and three-quarters, and, as far as we can judge from the descriptions, the MS. cannot be earlier than the eighth century; the three books, however, which are contained in it belong to a very early period: the Book of Enoch is at least of the first century, and may even be pre-Christian; the Gospel of Peter is, as we shall show presently, a product of the second century, and so is the Apocalypse of Peter. Strictly speaking, perhaps, we ought not to call the Enoch a new book, for the Ethiopic translation of it has long been known, as well as a few Greek fragments; but as the Ethiopic was made from the Greek, we have taken a step further back in the history of the work, and the recovery of a large part of the continuous Greek text is a very valuable aid to its knowledge and interpretation.

It is curious that the publication of this great discovery should have been so long delayed; the documents seem to have been found as far back as the winter of 1886-87, and there was certainly no need for five years' delay. But the reason of it is not far to seek. The French scholars, with some noble exceptions, are no longer interested in

Biblical and Patristic criticism; and it is evident that they did not, at first, realise what they had found. Certainly, if they had suspected its importance, we should have had some facsimile reproductions of the new text: the mathematical papyrus is given in complete facsimile; but the Gospel and the Apocalypse of Peter have not a line to show the style of the handwriting; they are not even honoured with a separate chapter or headline, but occur merely as a pendant to the text of Enoch. From all of which it is clear that we are fortunate in getting the text at all; it might have been laid aside in the Museum at Cairo as unimportant, and we might have waited, perhaps, another fifty years for our fragments of Peter. But we must not be ungrateful, for the vellum leaves are in the daylight now, and we shall certainly be able to get a facsimile text by-and-by.

Now, in the present pages we are concerned with the Gospel of Peter, and we shall dismiss the other two tracts with a few remarks. The Book of Enoch is, perhaps, the best representative of the canonical apocalyptic literature; as we have said, it probably leans on a pre-Christian base; it has certainly furnished material for the Epistle of Jude, who quotes it by name in the famous sentence beginning, "Behold the Lord cometh with ten thousand of his saints"; and if its date should be conclusively shown to be pre-Christian, it is probable that in some form or other it was a part of our Lord's own library. On these accounts, as well as because traces of its use are found in a number of early Christian fathers, it is a most important source from which the literature of a later period has drawn; and the recovery of so much of the Greek text is matter for much satisfaction.

The Apocalypse of Peter is a work, as we have said, which goes back at least as far as the second century, for traces of its use may be seen in many early documents. It was known to the martyrs of Carthage (the blessed Perpetua and her companions) as early as the year 203, and the descriptions which it contained of the bliss of the redeemed and the agonies of the lost have coloured the ideas and language of these martyrs. It must have been a very grotesque book, for the recovered portion gives details of the Inferno which rival Dante, without the significant under-current of moral teaching which redeems the great Italian Apocalypse. In the Apocalypse of Peter the retributive process is too obvious: false witnesses bite their own tongues in Gehenna, and have their mouths filled with fire; usurers stand up to their knees in a lake of pitch and blood and filth; those who blasphemed the way of righteousness are hung up by their tongues, and so on. It may, however, be taken for granted that this book, apocryphal as it no doubt is, having no connection with St. Peter, and having been rejected by the Church, exercised a wide influence over the imagination of the early Church, and made a broad mark on its literature.

And we may remark, before leaving this point and taking up the discussion of the Gospel of Peter, that what makes the recovery of early documents of every kind so important, is the fact that there is much more organic connection between early books than we have any idea of from the study of modern books. The materials which were at hand were always worked over by an author, who never suspected that in the nineteenth century we should call such a proceeding plagiarism; as a matter of fact, it was much more like piety than plagiarism; even the modern euphemism "newly-edited" was unknown. To rewrite a good author was a virtue, and it is to this feeling that we owe some of our best Patristic tracts, which are recognised to have some genealogical relation one to the other, as well as to incorporate common traditions. Possibly even Dante may have worked at the Apocalypse of Peter who shall say that he did not?

III

THE DOCETIC GOSPEL OF PETER.

CHAPTER III.

THE DOCETIC GOSPEL OF PETER.

THE reader will see a word at the head of this chapter which will perhaps look strange to him; but as he reads what we have to say it will become clear why we use the peculiar word.

We propose to ask the question, Was anything known before the excavations at Akhmîm concerning the Gospel of Peter? and were any quotations from it extant? Suppose an inquiring student had put the question a month ago, What is known about the Gospel of Peter? how should he have been answered?

In the first place, he would have been referred to a curious passage in the sixth book of the "Ecclesiastical History of Eusebius," where an account is given of the life and writings of Serapion, Bishop of Antioch; and he would find that Serapion had written, amongst other things, a tract against the Gospel which was circulated under the name of Peter; and, in the second place, he would be referred to the "Chronicle of Eusebius," where he would find the date of the appointment of Serapion to the See of Antioch given as A.D. 191; and this date cannot be very far wrong, if indeed it is wrong at all. The Gospel of Peter must, therefore, be a product of at least as early as the second century.

But this is not all, for Eusebius gives us some further particulars and some extracts from the discourse of Serapion, by which we learn the reason of his writing, which was as follows:—The brethren in the Church at Rhossus, a little town at Cilicia, were in the habit of using this Gospel of Peter in their services; and when Serapion paid them a visit, probably in the early years of his episcopate, he said something to them about the use of this Gospel, which appeared strange to him. The brethren maintained that there was no reason for timidity or contention over such a matter as the use of the Gospel in question, and Serapion, who was unfamiliar with its contents, let the matter drop, giving them permission to read it. Later on, however, he became uneasy about it, and sent to borrow the book from certain quarters where he heard that it was current, and an examination of it showed that the Gospel which the good people at Rhossus were quietly reading was a decidedly heretical production; so he sent word to Rhossus to say that he was coming to pay them another visit, and that they were to expect him shortly. For he had read the book, and found it contained much more than the right teaching of the Saviour; in fact, he perceived that they had fallen under the influence of Marcion the heretic and of the successors of the Docetists. Now, Serapion in these words described the Gospel of Peter as a Docetist production We must now show briefly what is meant by Docetism.

The word means "seeming" or "putative," and is applied to those persons who refused to believe in the reality of our Lord's incarnation or sufferings. It is one of the earliest of all Church heresies, and in the present day it is very hard for us to realise how widely it spread, nor how many forms the protest against the humanity of Jesus took. Explanation after explanation was invented to show that He did not really suffer. Some said that there was indeed a man Jesus, upon whom the superior Christ descended at his baptism, thus constituting him the son of God ("this day have I begotten thee"), but they went on to teach that at the Crucifixion the man Jesus was deserted by the Being who had descended upon him. Others explained that not even Jesus was crucified, but that the soldiers took Simon the Cyrenian by mistake and crucified him, while the real Jesus looked on and smiled. The variety of different explanations which were made shows how rooted was the idea that God could not possibly have anything to do immediately with matter, or with the sufferings of a material universe; if He seemed to make such contact, it was only in appearance. The suffering Christ was a phantom; not a hair of His head was touched, let alone a bone being broken. It need scarcely be said that such peculiar beliefs could not have arisen amongst people who looked on our Lord as the natural product of the life already in the world; yet Docetism is demonstrably one of the earliest heresies. It is in all probability the heresy which John combats in his Epistles where he speaks of people who do not believe that the Son of God had come *in the flesh.* The Ignatian Epistles, also, which must certainly belong some way back in the second century, and perhaps in the first twenty years of the century, show what a conflict was going on in Antioch and in Asia Minor over this question of the reality of Jesus Christ. "If," says Ignatius, "it were as certain persons who are godless, that is unbelievers, say, that He *suffered only in semblance*, being themselves mere semblance, why am I in bonds?"

We can, perhaps, attribute to the same influence the excision in certain copies of the Gospel of Luke of the two verses which describe our Lord's agony and bloody sweat. Such language was fatal to the Docetic view; but as it is still uncertain whether the passage in question is a late insertion or an early omission, we must not press this point as an illustration of the wide diffusion of Docetic views. But we have made a rough statement, at all events, of what those views were, and we can get some idea of what the heretical Gospel of Peter must have been like from the language of Serapion. Probably what we have said will suffice in answering the question as to what the Gospel must have been like before it was found. So we will only add that the fact of Serapion's finding the people of Rhossus so attached to their Gospel as to be unwilling to give it up would lead us to think that it could hardly have been recently introduced. In the matter of Church lesson-books people are always conservative. Witness the struggle which St. Jerome went through before his Vulgate was accepted, and even he never succeeded in banishing the Old Psalter; witness the continuance of the Old Psalter in the Church of England, and the objection to the substitution of the Revised Version for the Authorised (the last, however, is a case of intelligent judgment, as well as conservatism). So everything leads us to believe that the Gospel of Peter must have been written a good while before the year 190.

And now let us turn to the recovered Gospel, and see whether it shows any traces of heretical opinions, and, in particular, whether it is marked by Docetist tendencies. We will presently give the translation of the whole of the text which has been recovered. But first we draw the attention of the reader to the following points :—The recovered portion* belongs almost entirely to the close of the Gospel story, that part which contains the passion and resurrection of our Lord. Consequently we cannot verify or determine whether the author of the Gospel held any peculiar views with regard to our Lord's relations to His own family—as, for instance,

---

* From early catalogues of Church books we are able to infer that about half of the Gospel has been recovered.

whether the "brethren of the Lord" were His real brethren on the mother's side, or any question of that kind. Neither can we determine whether any fantastic interpretation was made of the account of our Lord's baptism, with its descending dove and voice from the throne; nor can we tell whether the writer agreed with Marcion in believing that there was something phenomenal about our Lord's appearance in the synagogue at Nazareth, as though He had just dropped from heaven. But we can verify that the writer did not believe in a suffering Saviour, for he tells us so expressly. "They crucified Him between two malefactors: but He Himself was silent, as one who felt no pain." Further, we find that, instead of the cry of Divine despair, which the Evangelists give from the Psalm in the words, "My God, my God, why hast thou forsaken me?" the writer has substituted the words, "My Power, my Power, thou hast forsaken me" (or, perhaps, as a question, "Hast thou forsaken me?"). Now, here he has either reverted to some other translation of the Psalms than that of the Septuagint, or he has deliberately changed the language of the canonical Gospels to suit his own beliefs. But one thing is clear: he is a Docetist, and the Power which has left the Lord is the Christ which had descended upon Him at some earlier time, probably at the Baptism. This, then, is our first reason for identifying the recovered fragment with the lost Gospel of Peter: it would be a sufficient reason of itself. And the Docetism is confirmed by remarking how the writer avoids every detail that implied suffering, such as the words "I thirst," and the account of the piercing of His side. But a further reason is conclusive, at all events. The Gospel story is written in the first person, and is the narrative of an eye-witness. For example, the writer says, "I and my fellows were grieved and wounded in heart, and we went away and hid ourselves, for we were being sought for by those evildoers [the Jews], on the ground that we were planning to burn the temple." Who is the person that speaks in this way of himself and his companions? Obviously he must be a distinguished figure in the circle of the Apostles. At the close of our fragment he tells his name: "I, Simon Peter, and Andrew, my brother, took our nets and went to the sea with Levi, the son of Alphæus, whom the Lord . . ." And here the fragment ends. But there is no room for hesitation that we are dealing with a Gospel that professed to be written in Peter's own name. So that we are sure that the book which Serapion condemned at the end of the second century has, in part, been recovered. Would that more of it had been found!

IV.

THE EXTANT TEXT OF THE NEW GOSPEL.

CHAPTER IV.

THE EXTANT TEXT OF THE NEW GOSPEL.

WE will now translate the portion of the new Gospel which has reached us. In doing so, it must be noted that, as the text has not been edited at all, but only transcribed, something must be done to correct the obvious mistakes of the copy and of the original. As a general rule, these mistakes are not more serious than a compositor's blunders, and may be readily corrected. Sometimes, however, they are more deeply-seated: where the original reading will not yield itself to critical inquiry, we shall mark the doubtful word with an asterisk. It will not, however, be possible to make any study of the corrections in such a tract as the present, which is only concerned with putting the new find before the general reader in the simplest form possible. It will be seen that we place, in the margin, the references to the canonical Gospels where the Gospel of Peter overlaps. A very little examination will show that the Scripture accounts have been very freely handled by the would-be Simon Peter. We shall show this more at length presently. Meanwhile it will be proper to put the references in the margin, so that a comparison with the English New Testament may indicate the extent to which the new Gospel agrees with the old.

Matt. xxvii. 24. But none of the Jews washed

their hands, neither did Herod, nor any of his judges, and when they would have washed them, Pilate rose up: and thereupon Herod the king bids that the Lord should be taken off, saying to them, Do with Him as I bade you do. And there was come thither Joseph, the friend of Pilate and of the Lord, and knowing that they are going to crucify
<small>Matt.xxvii.57. Mark xv. 42. Luke xxiii.50.</small> Him, he came to Pilate and begged the body of the Lord for burial.
<small>Luke xxiii. 7.</small> And Pilate sent to Herod and asked for His body; and Herod said, Brother Pilate, even if no one had asked for Him, we should have had to bury Him, for already
<small>Luke xxiii.54.</small> the Sabbath draws on: for it is written in the law that the sun

must not go down upon a murdered person, on the day before their feast, the feast of unleavened bread. But they who had taken the Lord were pushing Him along at a run, and saying, Let us hale the Son of God, now that we have Him in our power; and they clad Him with purple, and they seated Him on a seat of judgment, saying, Judge righteously, O King of Israel; and one of them brought a crown of thorns and set it upon the head of the Lord.

And others standing by spat on His face, and others again struck Him on the cheeks; others pricked Him with a reed, and some were scourging Him and saying, This is

THE EXTANT TEXT OF THE NEW GOSPEL. 45

the honour wherewith we will honour the Son of God. And _{Luke xxiii. 32.} _{John xix. 18.} they brought two malefactors and crucified the Lord between them. But He was silent, as if in no wise feeling pain; and when they set up the cross, they inscribed the words, "This is the King of Israel." And having laid down His _{John xix. 24.} _{Ps. xxii. 18.} garments before Him, they divided them and cast lots for them.

_{Matt. xxvii. 44.} _{Mark xv. 32.} _{Luke xxiii. 39.} But one of those malefactors reproached them, saying, We have suffered thus on account of the evil deeds which we did, but this man, who has become the Saviour of men, what evil has He done? and [the Jews,] being provoked at him, _{John xix. 31.} commanded that his legs should not

be broken, in order that he might die in torment. And it was now midday, and darkness covered all the land of Judæa, and they were troubled and in anxiety lest the sun should be setting, since He was yet alive; for it is written for them that the sun should not set upon a murdered man. And one of them said, Let us give Him to drink gall mingled with vinegar, and when they had mingled it, they gave Him to drink; and thus they brought all things to a fulfilment, and filled up the measure of their sins upon their own head. And many went about with lanterns, thinking that it was night,* and they fell down.* And the Lord cried out, saying,

> Matt.xxvii.45.
> Mark xv. 33.
> Luke xxiii. 44.

> Matt.xxvii.34.

THE EXTANT TEXT OF THE NEW GOSPEL. 47

Ps. xxii. 1. My Power, my Power, hast thou
Matt. xxvii. 51. forsaken me? And when He had
Mark xv. 38.
Luke xxiii. 45. said this He was taken up. And
the same hour the vail of the temple
of Jerusalem was rent in twain; and
then they drew out the nails from
the hands of the Lord, and laid Him
Matt. xxvii. 51. on the earth, and the earth was
wholly shaken, and great fear came
upon them. Then the sun shone
out, and it was found to be the
ninth hour. But the Jews rejoiced
Mark xv. 45. greatly, and gave the body to
Joseph to bury, for he had been
an observer of all the good deeds
which Jesus did. And he took
the Lord and washed Him, and
Mark xv. 46. wrapped Him in a linen cloth,
Matt. xxvii. 60.
John xix. 41. and brought Him into his own

tomb, which was called Joseph's Garden. Then the Jews and the elders and the priests, when they saw what an evil deed they had done to themselves, began to beat their breasts and to say, Woe to our sins, for the judgment and the end of Jerusalem is at hand.

And I with my companions was grieving, and, being wounded in heart, we hid ourselves, for we were sought for by them as malefactors and as men who wished to burn the temple. And we were fasting over all these things, and sitting down, grieving and weeping, night and day, until the Sabbath.

And the scribes and Pharisees and elders were gathered together,

THE EXTANT TEXT OF THE NEW GOSPEL. 49

for they had heard that all the people were murmuring and beating their breasts and saying, If such mighty signs are wrought at His death, consider how righteous a man He is! The elders were afraid and came to Pilate, beseeching him and saying, Give us soldiers, that we may guard His tomb for three days, lest His disciples come and steal Him away, and the people suppose that He is risen from the dead, and do us ill. And Pilate delivered to them Petronius the centurion with soldiers to guard the sepulchre; and with them there came elders and scribes to the sepulchre; and they with the centurion and the soldiers who were there all together rolled a

Luke xxiii. 47.

Matt. xxvii. 64.

Matt. xxvii. 66.

great stone and laid it at the door of the tomb, and they plastered seven seals, and pitched a tent there and mounted guard.

Luke xxiii. 54. And early in the morning, as the Sabbath was drawing on, there came a crowd from Jerusalem and from the surrounding country to see the tomb which had been sealed.

And in the night when the Lord's day was drawing on, as the soldiers were on guard, two and two in each watch, there was a great voice in heaven, and they saw the heavens

Luke xxiv. 4. opened, and two men descend thence with great radiance, and they stood over the tomb. But that stone which had been cast at the door rolled away of itself and withdrew to one side, and the tomb was opened, and both the young men entered.

_{Mark xvi. 5.}

When those soldiers saw this, they aroused the centurion and the elders (for they also were present on guard); and as they were relating what they had seen, again they behold three men coming out of the tomb, and two of them were supporting the third, and a cross was following them: and the heads of the two men reached to the heaven, but the head of Him who was being led along by them was higher than the heavens. And they heard a voice from heaven which said, Hast thou preached to them that are asleep? And a response was heard from the cross, Yea.

The watchers then deliberated amongst themselves as to going and making the thing known to Pilate: and while they were yet considering the matter the heavens appeared again open, and a man descended and entered into the tomb. When those who were with the centurion by night saw these things, they hurried to Pilate, leaving the sepulchre which they were guarding, and they related all which they had seen, being greatly distressed and Matt. xxvii. 54. saying, Truly this was the Son of Mark xv. 39. God. And Pilate answered and Matt. xxvii. 24. said to them, I am pure of the blood of the Son of God, but this deed was your good pleasure. Then they all drew near and besought him and entreated him to command the centurion and the soldiers to say nothing of what they had seen. For it is better for us, they said, to be guilty of the greatest sin in the sight of God, than to fall into the hands of the people of the Jews and be stoned. Pilate thereupon ordered the centurion and the soldiers to say nothing.

<small>Matt. xxviii. 1.
Mark xvi. 1.
Luke xxiv. 1.</small> And at the dawn of the Lord's day Mary Magdalene, a disciple of the Lord, who, being afeard of the Jews because they were inflamed by anger, had not done at the sepulchre as women were wont to do over the dead and those that were

beloved by them, took her friends with her and came to the tomb where He had been laid; and they were afraid lest the Jews should see them, and they said, Though we were not able to weep and to bewail Him in that day when He was crucified, yet now at the tomb let us do so.

Mark xvi. 3. But who shall roll us away the stone which was laid at the door of the tomb, that we may enter in, and sit by Him and do Him His
Mark xvi. 4. due? For the stone was a great one, and we are afraid lest some one should see us, and if we are not able [to carry out our plan], let us cast down at the door
Luke xxiv. 1. what we are carrying in remem-

THE EXTANT TEXT OF THE NEW GOSPEL. 55

brance of Him, and let us weep and wail until we reach our own homes.

And they came there and found the sepulchre opened; and drawing near thither, they stooped down, and they see a young man sitting in the midst of the sepulchre, beautiful and clad in a most dazzling robe, who said to them, Wherefore are ye come? whom do ye seek? Is it the one who was crucified? He is risen and gone; and if ye do not believe, stoop down and see the place where He was laid; for He is not here; for He is risen, and has gone to the place from whence He was sent.

<small>John xx. 5.</small>
<small>Mark xvi. 5.</small>

<small>Matt. xxviii. 5.</small>
<small>Mark xvi. 6.</small>

<small>Matt. xxviii. 6.</small>
<small>Mark xvi. 6.</small>

<small>Matt. xxviii.8.
Mark xvi. 8.</small> Then the women fled away in fear.

And it was the last day of the feast of unleavened bread, and many people were going [from the city] to their homes, the feast being ended. But we the twelve disciples of the Lord wept and grieved, and <small>John xx. 10.</small> each of us in grief at what had happened withdrew to his house. But I, Simon Peter, and Andrew, <small>John xxi. 3.</small> my brother, took our nets, and departed to the sea, and there was <small>Mark ii. 14.</small> with us also Levi, the son of Alphæus, whom the Lord

V.

ON THE SOURCES OF THE NEW GOSPEL.

CHAPTER V

ON THE SOURCES OF THE NEW GOSPEL.

WE come now to the interesting question of the sources from which the person who disguises himself as Peter has drawn in compiling his Gospel. The question is a peculiarly interesting one, because every student of the canonical Gospels knows that, behind the extant texts, there lies an amount of common matter, which might conceivably be traditional, but is almost certain to be some one or more books which have disappeared, but which are to some extent capable of restoration by critical processes. Moreover, there are many suggestions in the study of the early manuscripts, versions, and quotations of the canonical Gospels which lead us to believe that some collateral matter has occasionally influenced the tradition of the text: for example, when we find in one of the most famous copies of the Gospels a story about our Lord's reproving a man who was working on the Sabbath with the striking words, "Man, if thou knowest what thou doest, blessed art thou; but if thou knowest not, thou art accursed, and a transgressor of law"; it is not unnatural to suppose (of course, it is only a supposition) that some collateral account has been utilised to expand the narrative in the Gospel of Luke. But none of these extra-canonical gospels, or sources of gospels, have as yet come to light.

When, therefore, we do succeed in finding

a large portion of an extra-canonical gospel of early date, the first question that arises relates to its affinities with the canonical Gospels. So we must try, as far as the matter lies on the surface, to determine how the Gospel of Peter is related to Matthew, Mark, Luke, and John. Now, I suppose that a person who merely read the new Gospel over in English could come to certain conclusions immediately. He would not only be able to see that the Gospel was heretical in the sense of being Docetic, as we have explained above, but he would recognise that it was in many respects of a later period than the canonical Gospels. For example, the term "Lord's Day" is never used in the New Testament except in the first chapter of the Apocalypse ("I was in spirit in [or on] the Lord's Day"), but even here it is doubtful whether the writer means the Sunday or the Day of Judgment. In the Gospels it is called the First Day of the Week; and I think it is not until we come to the "Teaching of the Apostles" that we find the Christian usage of the term "Lord's Day" established. But since the Gospel of Peter uses the term freely, we can only infer that we have in the term an evidence of a later date.

The next thing that an English reader would notice would be the curious coincidences with points in the synoptic Gospels and St. John, which render it easy to show that Peter (whoever he was) has been drawing upon all four canonical Gospels. We will begin by showing that he uses the narrative of the Fourth Gospel.

The closing words of the fragment relate

to the departure of Simon Peter and Andrew, with Levi, the son of Alphæus, to the Sea of Galilee for the purpose of fishing. The writer is evidently thinking of the account in the last chapter of John where Simon Peter * says, "I go a fishing"; and the other disciples say, "We also go with thee." But either because he did not recall the previous verse in John, which says that there were with Peter both Thomas and Nathanael, James and John, and two other disciples, or else because he was making a hasty guess at the two nameless disciples, he has introduced Andrew and Levi, the son of Alphæus. Levi, the son of Alphæus, is only known from St. Mark's Gospel, which is suspicious of the use of Mark also. But for the present let us keep to the

---

* Note the agreement in the form of the name.

question of the employment of the Johannine account.

If we are right that the proposal to go fishing has been copied, we shall find some more traces. For example, in the account of the crucified malefactors we are told that one of them reviled the Jews, and that the Jews in revenge commanded that his legbones should not be broken, but that he should die in agony. Now, the only writer who mentions the breaking of the bones of the criminals is St. John. The false Peter knew the story and altered it, but he forgot to put in an explanation of the custom of breaking the legs of the crucified people; he assumed that his readers knew about it; in fact, he had already drawn upon the regulation which St. John reports, that the condemned persons should not hang upon the cross on the Sabbath, for that Sabbath was a high day, and had explained that the law prohibited that the sun should go down over a murdered person on the day before their feast, which is the feast of unleavened bread. This is his explanation of the "high day" of St. John, which certainly needed a note; it is not a satisfactory explanation, however, because it is not clear that the Crucifixion took place on the day before the Passover, nor that the Passover in St. John occurred on a Sabbath. It may be conjectured that the reason why the writer made up the story that one thief did not have his legs broken is due to the language of St. John ("they brake the legs of the first").

When the false Peter relates the entombment of the Lord, he says that Joseph buried the body in his own tomb, which was called Joseph's Garden. The only writer in the New Testament who mentions the garden is St. John: "In the place where He was crucified, there was a garden; and in the garden a new tomb."

The writer makes Mary Magdalene and the women *stoop down* and look into the tomb. The language shows that he has copied John xx. 5, where Peter stoops down and looks in. (This note of St. John appears also in the common text of Luke xxiv. 12, where it is, however, an addition borrowed from St. John.)

The detail that they crucified Jesus in the midst between the two robbers is from John xix. 18 ("Jesus in the midst"). The words "They clad Him with purple" are from John xix. 2 A more difficult passage is in the words "They seated Him on a seat of judgment," which occur in very nearly the same sense in Justin Martyr. It has been generally suspected that this expression arose out of a misunderstanding of John xix. 13, "Pilate brought Jesus forth, and sat on a judgment-seat," where the word "sat" has been taken transitively instead of intransitively, so as to mean, "Pilate brought Jesus forth, and sat Him on a judgment-seat." If this be the right explanation, we have the same mistake both in Justin and in the false Peter, and both of them employ the account in St. John.

From St. John also (xix. 1) comes the reference to the scourging ("Some of them were scourging Him"), and perhaps the casting of lots for His raiment. In the latter case, however, the language is a little peculiar, and it looks as if it might be taken from some unknown version of the Psalms (Psalm xxii. 18). Taking all these coincidences of language and ideas together (and it is probable that the illustrations might be extended), we consider it certain that our false Peter had a good acquaintance with St. John's Gospel.

Equally striking are the coincidences with the synoptic Gospels. The material is very freely handled, and the writer makes all sorts of fantastic combinations; but he leaves enough of the language in agreement with the originals to make identification of its sources comparatively easy. We will take only a few cases, as it is impossible to give the subject here the exhaustive treatment which it demands.

The opening words of the fragment imply that something had preceded about the washing of Pilate's hands before the people. This account is in Matt. xxvii. 24. The writer has enlarged upon it, by implying that Herod and the other judges were not allowed to wash their hands. His object was clearly to lay upon Herod and the Jews the infamy from which Pilate had judicially cleared himself.

The expression "vinegar mingled with gall" is probably from Matt. xxvii. 34, in which case it is in agreement with the Received Text against modern editors. The request for soldiers to guard the tomb comes from Matt. xxvii. 64, with which the words, "lest His disciples come and steal Him away, and the people suppose that He is risen from the dead," closely agree. In the same connection the obscure sentence of Matthew, "sealing the stone and setting a watch *along with the guard*," receives elucidation in the following manner: "The elders and scribes come to the sepulchre, and *with the centurion and the soldiers who were there all together* rolled a great stone," etc.

The reader will see throughout the account how dependent it is on the Gospel of Matthew. There are, of course, cases in which the synoptic tradition is so decidedly a unit that we cannot tell which Gospel is quoted, but the individualities of the separate accounts are very fairly represented.

When the women propose to cast down what they are carrying in remembrance of Him at the door of the sepulchre, there is nothing in the false Peter to intimate what they were carrying, but the single word "carrying" betrays Luke xxiv. 1: "They came to the tomb, carrying the spices which they had prepared." The false Gospel needs the canonical texts for its elucidation.

When the two men descend from heaven and stand over the tomb, we are following the tradition in Luke xxiv. 4 ("ló! two men stood over them in glistering raiment"); but when we are told that the tomb opened and the young men entered (no mention having been previously made that the angelic visitors were youthful in appearance), we are drawing on the "young man" of Mark xvi. 5. And, indeed, the writer seems to have made an attempt to harmonise the canonical accounts of the Resurrection; for the *two* angels carry Christ to Paradise, and afterwards the heavens open again, and *one* angel descends and sits in the tomb and converses with the women. This is ingenious, and seems to intimate that the difficulties in making a close and consistent harmony of the separate narratives were felt at a very early period.

Probably enough has been said to show the use of the four canonical Gospels, and the only question is whether the daring Docetist who concocted the book had access to other sources of information than these. It is hardly possible, as yet, before the book has been thoroughly handled by critics, to come to any very decided conclusion. Perhaps it will suffice to point out the directions in which the inquiry must be made. To this we will devote a separate chapter.

VI.

SOME UNCANONICAL PARALLELS TO THE GOSPEL OF PETER.

CHAPTER VI.

SOME UNCANONICAL PARALLELS TO THE GOSPEL OF PETER.

ONE of the first books to compare a recovered second-century gospel with is the famous Harmony of Tatian, to which we alluded in our introduction. We must see whether the two documents have anything in common, and then we must try to find out the reason for their agreement: as, for instance, whether Peter has used Tatian or Tatian Peter, or whether both of them are working upon common sources. We will first draw the reader's attention to a curious addition to the story of the Crucifixion which can be shown, with very high probability, to have once stood in the Harmony of Tatian. In some notes which I published a few years since on the Harmony of Tatian, I employed the method of combination of passages in different writers who were known to have used the Harmony, or different texts which were suspected of having borrowed from it, to show that in the account of the Crucifixion there stood a passage something like the following: "They beat their breasts and said, Woe unto us, for the things which are done to-day for our sins; for the desolation of Jerusalem hath drawn nigh." The way I arrived at this conclusion was by comparing the Syriac book called the Doctrine of Addai, which uses the text of Tatian, with the Syriac

Gospel of Cureton, which is closely related to Tatian, and with Ephrem the Syrian's commentary upon the text of Tatian. Perhaps the best way will be to transcribe a passage from my former published notes:—

"Our next illustration of an apocryphal saying in the Diatessaron is taken from Luke xxiii. 48. The verse in the Arabic Harmony follows on Matt. xxvii. 54 thus:— Matt. xxvii. 54: 'Truly this was the Son of God.' Luke xxiii. 48: 'And all the multitudes, who had come together for the sight, seeing what had happened, returned beating their breasts.'"

So far there is nothing that differs from our current texts; but when we turn to the Doctrine of **Addai**, we find the following passage, in which the connection of ideas needs to be carefully studied: "Unless those who crucified Him had known that He was the Son of God, they would not have had to proclaim the desolation of their city, nor would they have brought down Woe! upon themselves." Now, the author of the Doctrine of Addai used as his Biblical text-book the harmony made by Tatian, and we may detect in this passage a reference to the passage which the Diatessaron quotes from Matt. xxvii. 54; but there is nothing in what follows in the Arabic Harmony which suggests an allusion to the desolation of the city, or an imprecation upon or lamentation over themselves. Suppose, however, we turn to the Curetonian Syriac: here we have—

"Truly this man was just. And all those which were assembled there, and saw that which was done, were smiting upon their breast and saying, Woe to us, what is this! Woe to us for our sins!" (Luke xxiii. 47).

Here we have the connection which was wanting in the Arabic Harmony; and the same reading is found in the celebrated old Latin Codex of St. Germain (which contains a very early text of the Gospel of Matthew), and which reads,—

"Woe unto us, the things which are done to-day for our sins; for the desolation of Jerusalem hath drawn nigh."

Taking this with the Curetonian passage, we can restore the whole of the sequence which is found in the Doctrine of Addai. But that Addai took it from the Diatessaron, and not from the old Syriac of Cureton, is evident, not only from what we know of its own allusions to the Diatessaron, but also from the fact that it does not say "This was a just man," as all MSS. do in *Luke*, but "This was truly the Son of God," as it runs in Matthew. We can therefore restore the missing sentences to the Diatessaron; and if any doubt remained in our minds, it would be dispelled by turning to Ephrem's commentary on the Harmony, where we find as follows: "*Woe unto us, woe unto us, this was the Son of God.* . . . When the Sun of righteousness had appeared, purifying the lepers and opening the eyes of the blind, by that light the blind men did not recognise that the King of the city of Jerusalem had come. But when the natural sun had failed them, then by the darkness it became transparent to them that *the destruction of their city had come.* The judgments of the desolation of Jerusalem, saith He, are come."

Now, the reader will be interested to see

that the missing sentence which I restored to Tatian's text has turned up in the Gospel of Peter, for we read that "the Jews and the elders and the priests, when they saw what an evil deed they had done to themselves, began to beat their breasts and to say, Woe to our sins, for the judgment and the end of Jerusalem is at hand."

Did the false Peter take this from Tatian, or was it the other way? or did both of them use some uncanonical writing or tradition?

We will show one or two more cases in which the text of our fragment approaches to the text of Tatian, or to that of the writers who depend directly upon Tatian.

The language of the fragment, "Then the sun shone out, and it was found to be the ninth hour," should be compared with that of Ephrem, Tatian's commentator: "Three hours the sun was darkened, and afterwards it shone out again."

The Docetic quotation from the Psalms "My Power, my Power, hast thou forsaken me?" is peculiar in this respect, that the second possessive pronoun is wanting, so that we ought to translate it, "Power, my Power." In using only one possessive pronoun, the writer agrees with the Septuagint text of the Psalms against the text as quoted in the canonical Gospels. Now, it is curious that Tatian's text had a similar peculiarity, for Ephrem gives it as "God, my God," and the Arabic Harmony as *Yaiil, Yaiili*, where the added suffix belongs to the possessive pronoun. This is a remarkable coincidence, and makes one suspect that Tatian had "Power, my Power" in his text, and that it has been corrected away. And it is significant that Ephrem, in commenting on the passage, says, "The divinity did not so depart from the humanity as to be cut off from it, but only as regards the *power* of the divinity, which was hidden both from the Slain and the slayers." This looks very suspicious that Ephrem found something in his text of Tatian differing from the words "God, my God."

Another case of parallelism is in the speech of the angel to Mary: "He is not here, for He is risen, *and has gone away to the place from whence He was sent.*" At first sight this looks like a wilful expansion on the part of the writer of the Gospel, but on a reference to the Persian father Aphrahat, who is more than suspected of having used the text of Tatian, we find the words, "And the angels said to Mary, He is risen and gone away to Him that sent Him," which is very nearly in coincidence with the text of the false Peter. These coincidences will need to be very carefully examined, in order that we may see whether Peter has really drawn upon the Tatian text in the composition of his Gospel. A number of points will need to be looked into in connection with this. For example, the sequence of the narrative of Peter, which is often contrary to the canonical Gospels, will have to be examined side by side with the sequence of the Harmony.

There is another possible source that suggests itself: a comparison of the text of Peter with the writings of Justin Martyr will betray one or two very remarkable coincidences, and the question will be asked, What is the meaning of them?

For example, the Gospel of Peter tells us

SOME UNCANONICAL PARALLELS. 85

that those who had apprehended the Lord pushed Him along at a run, and said, "Let us hale the Son of God, since we have Him in our power, . . . and they set Him on the judgment-seat and said, Judge righteously, O King of Israel."

Now, Justin tells us that in fulfilment of the prophecies concerning Jesus the Jews "haled Him, and set Him on a judgment-seat, and said, Judge for us." It is clear that the writer of the Gospel is working from the same ground as Justin, unless we choose to say that Justin copied Peter, which does not look at all probable on the face of things.

A somewhat similar instance is in the language describing the casting of lots for our Lord's vesture, where the writer of the Gospel uses a very peculiar word for "lots," which is also employed by Justin in his Dialogue with Trypho, where he speaks of the same occurrence.

I think the real explanation of these coincidences is that both Justin and Peter had a little text-book of fulfilled prophecies, to be used in discussions with Jews. These Old Testament prophecies were taken from a Greek version, which was not the Septuagint, but was probably the version of Aquila the Jew, or some distinctly Jewish version. And I suspect that the expression "Let us hale the Son of God" comes from the third chapter of Isaiah, in a verse where the Hebrew reads "Say ye to the righteous," but the Septuagint reads "Let us bind the righteous," and, according to my idea, some other early translation had "Let us hale the righteous." The text of the passage in Isaiah varied much in early times. The early Christian writers were very keen in reading the New Testament into the Old and the Old into the New. They found New Testament interpretations where we should never see anything of the kind.

But this is a subject which will demand a good deal more examination. So we will only say that, if our suspicions are correct, it ought to be possible by-and-by to find the place in the second century to which Peter must be referred with a very good degree of accuracy. He may turn out to be between Tatian and Serapion, and nearer to the former than the latter; or he may be between the time of the translator Aquila (in the reign of Hadrian) and the time of Serapion.

Before concluding this chapter, we may ask ourselves one more question: Are there any traces of the use of any other of the canonical books? The only direction in which I can see the use of the New Testament outside of the Gospels is in some traces of the Apocalypse. Twice there is a suggestion of this: once in the sealing of the stone with seven seals, which is an imitation of the book with seven seals in Apoc. iv.; and again in the fabulous narration that the Cross followed Christ into Paradise. The explanation of this lies in the fact that all the early interpreters, Christians and Gnostics alike, held the Cross to be the tree of life, which brought redemption from the curse introduced by the tree of knowledge. It would be superfluous to quote proofs of this doctrine of Salvation by the Tree: we might fill pages with it. But since the Apocalypse uses the expression "the tree of life which is in the Paradise of my

God," it was counted proper that the Cross should ascend to Paradise when the Lord did. It is possible, however, to make the connection of ideas from the account of Paradise in the Book of Genesis, without the intervention of the Apocalypse. These are the only cases which I have noted where the suspicion is aroused as to the use of any other of the books of the New Testament beside the Gospels.

VII.

CONCLUDING REMARKS.

CHAPTER VII.

CONCLUDING REMARKS.

IT will have been remarked that the attitude of the writer is very unfriendly to the Jews; he is not only a foreigner as regards Palestine (as witness his calling the temple, the temple *of Jerusalem*), but he is an antagonistic foreigner. He expressly excepts Herod and the Jews from any washing of hands in token of innocence. He makes one of the crucified thieves reproach them for their treatment of the Saviour, and the Jews retaliate barbarously. The giving the draught of gall and vinegar is a crime which fills up their tale of sins. They are made to call down a special woe upon themselves and their city. They plot to kill the disciples on the plea that they are plotting to burn the city. All of these details are decidedly anti-Judaic; and we see that this is a later stage of Docetism than is combated in the Ignatian Epistles, where the Gnostic element with which Ignatius contends is Jewish in cast. In fact, Ignatius has to remind the Churches to which he writes that "Christianity did not believe in Judaism, but Judaism in Christianity." We can hardly refer the hostile feeling which would make a writer say that it was better to be guilty of any and every sin against God rather than to fall into the hands of the Jews to the early years of the second century.

So also with regard to the other Gnostic touches in the book, such as the enormous height of the angels, and still more so of the Christ. No doubt these are second-century details, since we find early Gnostic writings, such as the apocryphal Acts of John, to be coloured by them; and even in Perpetua's vision | the judge overtops the amphitheatre. But it can hardly be the early years of the second century when these legendary details were being developed.

Our text also contains the doctrine of the preaching to the spirits in prison, which was a very popular second-century doctrine, especially amongst Gnostics and Marcionites, and in some form goes back into the first century; but in our story the significance is that the Cross answers the question, "Hast thou preached to the sleepers?" The reason for this probably lies in the legendary doctrine that when Christ descended to Hades

He took the Cross with Him; thus the preaching in question was a preaching of the Cross. And certainly the early legends on the Descent into Hades give a very prominent place to the Cross. But it is again doubtful whether this development of the doctrine can be referred to the earlier years of the second century.

But it is time to bring these straggling and imperfect remarks to a conclusion. We have tried to present to our readers some idea of what a heretical gospel was like, judging from the first specimen of any length that has come to light. In the coming years we may hope and expect to find much more of the same kind, but we do not think that the first specimen is likely to produce the impression that the canonical Gospels are merely an ecclesiastical survival from a mass of similar literature, of nearly the same value as themselves. If the rest of the early gospel-makers who produced non-canonical texts were like our Docetist, we can only say that they were wanting, not merely in regard for truth and reverence for the subjects which they handled, but in every other quality which makes history possible. And we can quite understand the force of Hermas' allegorical conception, when he maintained the Church to be like a lady seated firmly on an ivory chair *with four legs*; and however fantastic the fathers of the second century may have been, we can see the reasonableness of their reiteration that the Gospels are four in number, like the winds of heaven and the pillars of the earth—not less than four, nor more than four, nor other than the approved and tested four.

PRINTED BY
HAZELL, WATSON, AND VINEY, LD.,
LONDON AND AYLESBURY.

BY THE SAME AUTHOR.

VOL. I. OF

The Devotional Library.
MEMORANDA SACRA.

Post 8vo, 3s. 6d.

CONTENTS.

God the God of the Living.

Believing and Becoming.

Gleaming as Crystal.

Heart Enlargement.

He Restoreth my Soul.

Addition and Multiplication.

A Conference on Death.

Christ will take all.

Strong Crying.

The Sentinel of the Heart.

Thy Father in Secret.

Tests of Faith, Love, and Rightness.

The Eternal Idea.

More Light Over.

Overcoming.

HODDER & STOUGHTON'S
NEW AND RECENT BOOKS.

THE FOURTH GOSPEL:
Evidences External and Internal Johannean Authorship.

By the late Right Rev. *J. B. LIGHTFOOT*, D.D., Bishop of Durham; the late Rev. *EZRA ABBOT*, D.D.; and the Rev. *ANDREW P. PEABODY*, D.D.

8vo, cloth, 7s. 6d.

"Among recent works in the department of Introduction none will be more highly prized than this volume."—*Expositor*.

THE APOSTLE PAUL:
A Sketch of the Development of his Doctrine.

By *A. SABATIER*, Professor in the Faculty of Protestant Theology in Paris. Translated from the French. Edited, with an additional Essay, by GEORGE G. FINDLAY, B.A.

Crown 8vo, cloth, 7s. 6d.

"The treatment throughout is well informed, sagacious, and though simple, we might say elementary, not by any means superficial. The translation has been carefully executed. I have sincere pleasure in confidently recommending the book as one which ministers and others will find to be a most useful addition to their library."—*Rev. Professor A. B. Bruce, D.D., in the "Modern Church."*

THE CHRISTIAN MINISTRY:
Its Origin, Constitution, Nature, and Work.

By the Very Rev. *WILLIAM LEFROY*, D.D., Dean of Norwich.

In One Volume. 8vo, cloth, 14s.

"In presenting his own views, which he does with remarkable power, and in the most lucid way, the author has occasion to controvert the opinions of several recent writers, a duty which he performs with great ability, fairness, and unvarying courtesy. These lectures show ripe scholarship, and a thorough mastery of materials by which a judgment is to be formed."—*Scotsman*.

THE EXPOSITOR'S BIBLE.

EDITED BY REV.

W. ROBERTSON NICOLL, M.A., LL.D.

FIRST SERIES.

Price 7s. 6d. each Volume.

THE BOOK OF GENESIS.

By the Rev. Professor *MARCUS DODS, D.D.*

SIXTH EDITION.

THE FIRST BOOK OF SAMUEL.
THE SECOND BOOK OF SAMUEL.

By the Rev. Professor *W. G. BLAIKIE, D.D., LL.D.*

FOURTH EDITION, TWO VOLS.

"Very full of suggestive thought."—*English Churchman.*
"A solid and able piece of work."—*Academy.*

THE GOSPEL OF ST. MARK.

By the Very Rev. *G. A. CHADWICK, D.D.*, Dean of Armagh.

FOURTH EDITION.

"This exposition is original, full of life, striking, and relevant. He has given us the fruit of much careful thought."—*British Weekly.*

THE EPISTLES TO THE COLOSSIANS AND PHILEMON.

By the Rev. *ALEXANDER MACLAREN, D.D.*

FIFTH EDITION.

"In nothing Dr. Maclaren has written is there more of beauty, of spiritual insight, or of brilliant elucidation of Scripture. Indeed, Dr. Maclaren is here at his best."—*Expositor.*

THE EPISTLE TO THE HEBREWS.

By the Rev. Principal *T. C. EDWARDS, D.D.*

FOURTH EDITION.

"There is abundant evidence of accurate scholarship, acute criticism, patient thought, and faculty of lucid exposition. However thoroughly any one has studied the Epistle here explained, he will certainly find in Dr. Edwards' volume fresh suggestions."—*Dr. Marcus Dods.*

THE EXPOSITOR'S BIBLE.

SECOND SERIES.

Price 7s. 6d. each Volume.

THE BOOK OF ISAIAH.
Vol. I. Chapters I.-XXXIX.
By the Rev. GEORGE ADAM SMITH, M.A.
SIXTH EDITION.

"This is a very attractive book. Mr. George Adam Smith had evidently such a mastery of the scholarship of his subject that it would be a sheer impertinence for most scholars, even though tolerable Hebraists, to criticise his translations. . . . A lucid, impressive, and vivid study of Isaiah."—*Spectator.*

THE EPISTLE TO THE GALATIANS.
By the Rev. Professor G. G. FINDLAY, B.A.
THIRD EDITION.

"In this volume we have the mature results of broad and accurate scholarshi , exegetical tact, and a firm grasp of the great principles underlying the Gospel of Paul presented in a form so lucid and attractive that every thoughtful reader can enjoy it."—*Dr. Beet.*

THE EPISTLES OF ST. JOHN.
By the Right Rev. W. ALEXANDER, D.D., D.C.L., Lord
Bishop of Derry and Raphoe.
SECOND EDITION.

"Full of felicities of exegesis. . . Brilliant and valuable."—*Literary Churchman.*

FIRST EPISTLE TO CORINTHIANS.
By the Rev. Professor MARCUS DODS, D.D.
THIRD EDITION.

"Dr. Dods' writings are always excellent, and the one before us is no exception to the rule."—*Record.*

THE BOOK OF REVELATION.
By the Rev. Professor W. MILLIGAN, D.D.
SECOND EDITION.

"Dr. Milligan's scholarly and attractive exposition."—*Aberdeen Free Press.*

THE PASTORAL EPISTLES.
By the Rev. ALFRED PLUMMER, D.D., Durham.
THIRD EDITION.

"The treatment is throughout scholarlike, lucid, thoughtful."—*Guardian.*

THE EXPOSITOR'S BIBLE.

THIRD SERIES.

Price 7s. 6d. each Volume.

THE GOSPEL OF ST. MATTHEW.
By the Rev. *J. MONRO GIBSON, D.D.*

SECOND EDITION.

"This running commentary upon St. Matthew's Gospel sets before the reader our Lord's words, deeds, and sufferings as recorded by that Evangelist in a vivid light."—*Guardian.*

THE BOOK OF EXODUS.
By the Very Rev. *G. A. CHADWICK, D.D.*

SECOND EDITION.

"This is, to a great extent, a model of what an expository commentary should be. To exhibit the Old Testament in the light of the New, and to point out the spiritual and permanent truth under the type by which it was in that early age expressed, and through which it still shines, cannot fail to render a commentary extremely valuable."—*Literary Churchman.*

JUDGES AND RUTH.
By the Rev. *R. A. WATSON, M.A.*, Author of "Gospels of Yesterday."

"This is an unusually attractive volume. His pages will give many a valuable hint to the preacher."—*Literary Churchman.*

THE GOSPEL OF ST. LUKE.
By the Rev. *HENRY BURTON, M.A.*

"His chapters are full of vivid illustration, and fresh, bright exposition."—*Record.*

THE PROPHECIES OF JEREMIAH.
With a Sketch of His Life and Times.

By the Rev. *C. J. BALL, M.A.*, Chaplain of Lincoln's Inn.

"The critical portion will be prized most as it exhibits deep learning, breadth of view, and clear insight into the prophet's meaning."—*Manchester Examiner.*

THE BOOK OF ISAIAH.
Vol. II. By the Rev. *GEORGE ADAM SMITH, M.A.*

SECOND EDITION.

"The results of thorough scientific study are here presented, not as the bare and wintry stem which too often repels, but rich and attractive, with the foliage and fruit which sound criticism yields."—*Dr. Marcus Dods.*

THE EXPOSITOR'S BIBLE.

FOURTH SERIES.

Price 7s. 6d. each Volume.

THE GOSPEL OF ST. JOHN. VOL. I.

By the Rev. *MARCUS DODS*, D.D., Professor of Exegetical Theology, New College, Edinburgh.

"An excellent contribution to the series. Dr. Dods has the gift of lucidity of expression."—*Guardian*.

THE EPISTLES OF ST. JAMES AND ST. JUDE.

By Rev. *A. PLUMMER*, D.D., Master of University College, Durham.

"It is even a better piece of work than his former volume on the Pastoral Epistles. It contains everything that the student can desire by way of introduction to the two Epistles, while for those who read with an eye to the manufacture of sermons, or for their own edification, the doctrinal and moral lessons are developed in a style redolent of books, yet singularly easy and unaffected. Points of interest abound."—*Saturday Review*.

THE BOOK OF ECCLESIASTES.

With a New Translation.

By the Rev. *SAMUEL COX*, D.D.

"The most luminous, original, and practical exposition of Ecclesiastes which is within the reach of ordinary English readers."—*Speaker*.

THE BOOK OF PROVERBS.

By the Rev. *R. F. HORTON*, M.A., Hampstead.

"In each of these lectures will be found much strong and vigorous thought, firm and logical reasoning, and the results of high culture and ability."—*Literary Churchman*.

THE BOOK OF LEVITICUS.

By the Rev. *S. H. KELLOGG*, D.D., Author of "The Light of Asia and the Light of the World."

"He has certainly succeeded in investing with fresh interest this old book of laws, with whose spirit he seems so heartily in sympathy."—*Scotsman*.

THE ACTS OF THE APOSTLES. VOL. I.

By the Rev. Professor *G. T. STOKES*, D.D.

"A very valuable addition to Biblical literature."—*British Weekly*.

THE EXPOSITOR'S BIBLE.

FIFTH SERIES, 1891-92.
Price 7s. 6d. each Volume.

The Book of Job.
By the Rev. R. A. WATSON, D.D., Author of "Gospels of Yesterday," etc.

The Epistles to the Thessalonians.
By the Rev. JAMES DENNEY, B.D.

The Psalms. Vol. I.
By the Rev. ALEXANDER MACLAREN, D.D.

The Acts of the Apostles. Vol. II.
By the Rev. Professor G. T. STOKES, D.D.

The Epistle to the Ephesians.
By the Rev. Professor G. G. FINDLAY, B.A.

The Gospel of St. John. Vol. II.
By the Rev. Professor MARCUS DODS, D.D.

SIXTH SERIES, 1893. *Preparing.*

The Epistle to the Philippians.
By the Rev. Principal RAINY, D.D.

The First Book of Kings.
By the Venerable F. W. FARRAR, D.D., Archdeacon of Westminster.

The Book of Joshua.
By the Rev. Professor W. G. BLAIKIE, D.D., LL.D.

The Book of Psalms. Vol. II.
By the Rev. ALEXANDER MACLAREN, D.D.

The Book of Daniel.
By the Rev. Professor J. M. FULLER, M.A.

Ezra, Nehemiah, and Esther.
By the Rev. Professor W. F. ADENEY, M.A.

The Foreign Biblical Library.

NOW COMPLETE.

Price 7s. 6d. each Volume.

BY PROFESSOR DELITZSCH, D.D.

I.
A BIBLICAL COMMENTARY ON THE PROPHECIES OF ISAIAH.

Authorised Translation from the Third Edition by the Rev. *JAMES DENNEY, B.D.*

In Two Volumes.

II.
A BIBLICAL COMMENTARY ON THE PSALMS.

Translated by Rev. *DAVID EATON, M.A.,* from the Latest Edition revised by the Author.

In Three Volumes.

"We heartily welcome this accurate translation of an indispensable work. Delitzsch's revised editions are so full of minute and interesting corrections and additions that his exegetical masterpieces deserve to be retranslated."—*Academy.*

SELECTED SERMONS OF SCHLEIERMACHER.

With a Biographical Sketch.

Translated by *MARY F. WILSON.*

In One Volume.

"The twenty-seven sermons chosen include fine examples of Schleiermacher's power."—*Manchester Examiner.*

The Foreign Biblical Library.

(CONTINUED.)

Price 7s. 6d. each Volume.

BY RICHARD ROTHE.
STILL HOURS.

With Introductory Essay by Rev. *J. MACPHERSON, M.A.*
Translated by *J. T. STODDART.*

In One Volume.

"It is a book of the first order, full of Rothe himself, and of which one wearies as little as of the face of a friend."—*Dr. Marcus Dods.*

BY PROFESSOR KURTZ.
CHURCH HISTORY.

Authorised Translation from the Latest Revised Edition, by the Rev. *JOHN MACPHERSON, M.A.*

In Three Volumes.

"The complete work of Professor Kurtz is now translated, and it really shows itself so improved in form, so much fuller in substance—in fact, so much changed in mind, body, and state, that it may claim to be a new history altogether."—*Scotsman.*

BY PROF. BERNHARD WEISS, Ph.D.
A MANUAL OF INTRODUCTION TO THE NEW TESTAMENT.

Translated by *A. J. K. DAVIDSON.*

In Two Volumes.

"As a thoroughly complete and satisfactory introduction from the point of view of a fairly conservative criticism, no book can compete with Weiss. It is throughout full of knowledge, of sense, and of vigour."—*Expositor.*

THE CLERICAL LIBRARY.

Price 6s. each Volume.

I.

THREE HUNDRED OUTLINES OF SERMONS ON THE NEW TESTAMENT.

"Will come as a godsend to many an overworked preacher."—*Ecclesiastical Gazette.*

II.

OUTLINES OF SERMONS ON THE OLD TESTAMENT.

"Excellently well done. The discourses of the most eminent divines of the day are dissected, and their main thoughts presented in a very compact and suggestive form."—*Methodist Recorder.*

III.

PULPIT PRAYERS BY EMINENT PREACHERS.

"The prayers are, in all cases, exceedingly beautiful, and cannot fail to be read with interest and profit, apart from the special purpose in view."—*Rock.*

IV.

OUTLINE SERMONS TO CHILDREN.

With Numerous Anecdotes.

"Nearly a hundred sermons, by twenty-nine eminent men. They are remarkably well written, and most interesting."—*Rock.*

V.

ANECDOTES ILLUSTRATIVE OF NEW TESTAMENT TEXTS.

"This is one of the most valuable books of anecdote that we have ever seen. There is hardly one anecdote that is not of first-rate quality."—*Christian Leader.*

VI.

EXPOSITORY SERMONS ON THE OLD TESTAMENT.

"Sermons of very unusual merit, requiring from us emphatic praise."—*Literary Churchman.*

THE CLERICAL LIBRARY.

Price 6s. each Volume.

VII.
EXPOSITORY SERMONS ON THE NEW TESTAMENT.

"These sermons, collected together from the best sources, represent the ablest among our public orators."—*Irish Ecclesiastical Gazette.*

VIII.
PLATFORM AIDS.

"Just the book to give to some overworked pastor."—*Christian.*

IX.
NEW OUTLINES OF SERMONS ON THE NEW TESTAMENT.

By *EMINENT PREACHERS.*

Hitherto unpublished.

"They have a freshness and vivacity which are specially taking."—*Sword and Trowel.*

X.
ANECDOTES ILLUSTRATIVE OF OLD TESTAMENT TEXTS.

"An excellent selection, likely to prove most useful to preachers."—*English Churchman.*

XI.
NEW OUTLINES OF SERMONS ON THE OLD TESTAMENT.

"Not only are they excellent specimens of condensed sermons, but hardly without exception they are striking, vigorous, and fresh in treatment and in thought."—*Literary World.*

XII.
OUTLINES OF SERMONS FOR SPECIAL OCCASIONS.

By *EMINENT PREACHERS.*

"Sermons from such miscellaneous sources could hardly fail to be varied and comprehensive as these undoubtedly are, nor could they fail to exhibit eloquence, originality, or spirituality."—*Rock.*

THE SERMON BIBLE.

Each Volume containing upwards of Four Hundred Sermon Outlines, and Several Thousand References.

Strongly bound in half buckram.   Price 7s. 6d. each Volume.

VOLUME I. **GENESIS TO 2 SAMUEL.**

„ II. **1 KINGS TO PSALM LXXVI.**

„ III. **PSALM LXXVII. TO THE SONG OF SOLOMON.**

„ IV. **ISAIAH TO MALACHI.**

„ V. **ST. MATTHEW I. TO XXI.**

„ VI. **ST. MATTHEW XXII. TO ST. MARK XVI.**

„ VII. **ST. LUKE I. TO ST. JOHN III.**

„ VIII. **ST. JOHN IV. TO ACTS VI.**

„ IX. **ACTS VI. TO 1 CORINTHIANS.**

„ X. **2 CORINTHIANS TO PHILIPPIANS.**

THE SERMON BIBLE.

OPINIONS OF THE PRESS.

"A very complete guide to the sermon literature of the present day."—*Scotsman.*

"The most practically useful work of its kind."—*Literary Churchman.*

"An excellent guide to the best English sermons of recent time."—*Methodist Recorder.*

"Admirable epitomes of the best homiletic literature."—*London Quarterly Review.*

"Beyond question the richest treasury of modern homiletics."—*Christian Leader.*

"Rich in variety, and thorough without being overloaded." *Rock.*

"A rich mine of homiletical wealth."—*Christian.*

"A truly valuable book for preachers."—*Church Bells.*

"Of unique excellence as a pulpit help."—*Baptist.*

"The editor of this work has rendered a valuable service by his keen and logical analysis of the sermons, his succinct statement of their main points, and his effective presentation of their more striking and essential thoughts."—*Baptist Magazine.*

"The plan has been carried out with such admirable impartiality, and such excellent taste, that the student who wishes to ascertain how a given text has been handled by the ablest English-speaking pulpit expositors of the day can hardly fail to find here what he seeks presented in the briefest form possible."—*Manchester Examiner.*

The Theological Educator.

Fcap. 8vo, 2s. 6d. each Volume.

AN INTRODUCTION TO THE OLD TESTAMENT.

By the Rev. C. H. H. WRIGHT, D.D.

"The work is of brief compass, and covers a vast field of study, but the necessary compression has been done with the skill of one experienced in the needs of students."—*Scotsman.*

THE WRITERS OF THE NEW TESTAMENT.

Their Style and Characteristics.

By the Rev. WILLIAM HENRY SIMCOX, M.A.

"One of the choicest productions of English scholarship in recent years."—*Manchester Examiner.*

THE LANGUAGE OF THE NEW TESTAMENT.

BY THE SAME AUTHOR.

"The most living grammar of the New Testament we have."—*Expositor.*

OUTLINES OF CHRISTIAN DOCTRINE.

By the Rev. H. C. G. MOULE, M.A.

AN INTRODUCTION TO THE NEW TESTAMENT.

By the Rev. Professor MARCUS DODS, D.D.

"Dr. Marcus Dods has packed away an immense amount of information in a very small space."—*Methodist Recorder.*

An Introduction to
THE TEXTUAL CRITICISM OF THE NEW TESTAMENT.

By the Rev. Professor B. B. WARFIELD, D.D.

"A masterly survey of the whole subject."—*Expositor.*

The Theological Educator.

Price 2s. 6d. each Volume.

A MANUAL OF CHURCH HISTORY.

By the Rev. *A. C. JENNINGS, M.A.*

In Two Volumes.

Vol. I.—From the First to the Tenth Century.
Vol. II.—From the Eleventh to the Nineteenth Century.

"They are small, but they include 'infinite riches in little room.'"—*Globe.*

A MANUAL OF CHRISTIAN EVIDENCES.

By the Rev. Prebendary *C. A. ROW, M.A.*

"A veritable *multum in parvo*, clear, cogent, and concise."—*Saturday Review.*

A MANUAL OF THE BOOK OF COMMON PRAYER.

Showing its History and Contents. For the use of those Studying for Holy Orders and others.

By the Rev. *CHARLES HOLE, B.A.*, King's College, London.

"It is not overloaded with detail, and yet supplies in an admirably compact shape all essential information."—*British Weekly.*

A HEBREW GRAMMAR.

By the Rev. *W. H. LOW, M.A.*, Joint Author of "A Commentary on the Psalms," etc., etc.

"A brief and masterly sketch of Hebrew grammar."—*Literary Churchman.*

AN EXPOSITION OF THE APOSTLES' CREED.

By the Rev. *J. E. YONGE, M.A.*, late Fellow of King's College, Cambridge.

"An able treatise."—*Church Times.*
"A handy book for divinity students, which will give them all the information they want for examination for Orders on the subject which it handles."—*Saturday Review.*

The Household Library of Exposition.

THE GALILEAN GOSPEL.
By Professor *A. B. BRUCE, D.D.*
THIRD THOUSAND.
Price 3s. 6d.

"We heartily commend this little volume as giving an outline ably drawn of the teaching of Christ."—*Spectator.*

THE SPEECHES OF THE HOLY APOSTLES.
By *DONALD FRASER, D.D.*
SECOND THOUSAND.
Price 3s. 6d.

"Exceedingly well done."—*Scottish Review.*

THE LAMB OF GOD.
Expositions in the Writings of St. John.
By *W. ROBERTSON NICOLL, M.A., LL.D.*
Price 2s. 6d.

"A volume of rare beauty and excellence."—*New York Independent.*

THE LORD'S PRAYER.
By *CHARLES STANFORD, D.D.*
THIRD THOUSAND.
Price 3s. 6d.

"For spiritual grasp and insight, for wealth of glowing imagery, and for rare felicity of style, it will hold a first place in this valuable series of expository monographs."—*Christian.*

THE LAST SUPPER OF OUR LORD,
And His Words of Consolation to the Disciples.
By *J. MARSHALL LANG, D.D.,* Barony Church, Glasgow.
THIRD THOUSAND.
Price 3s. 6d.

"With a rare power of insight—the result, doubtless, of much inward experience—Dr. Lang has entered into the very inmost spirit of the scenes and incidents, the words and feelings, which make up the history of that night."—*Scotsman.*

The Household Library of Exposition.
(*CONTINUED.*)

THE LAW OF THE TEN WORDS.
By *J. OSWALD DYKES, D.D.*
Crown 8vo. Price 3s. 6d.

"His style is a singular combination of strength and beauty."—*Literary World.*

THE LIFE OF DAVID.
As Reflected in His Psalms.
By *ALEXANDER MACLAREN, D.D.*, of Manchester.
SEVENTH EDITION.
Price 3s. 6d.

"Just the book we should give to awaken a living and historical interest in the Psalms."—*Guardian.*

THE TEMPTATIONS OF CHRIST.
By *G. S. BARRETT, M.A.*
Price 3s. 6d.

"Marked alike by careful language and sober thought."—*Guardian.*

THE PARABLES OF OUR LORD.
As Recorded by St. Matthew.
By *MARCUS DODS, D.D.*
SEVENTH THOUSAND.
Price 3s. 6d.

"There is certainly no better volume on the subject in our language." *Glasgow Mail.*

THE PARABLES OF OUR LORD.
As Recorded by St. Luke.
By *MARCUS DODS, D.D.*
SIXTH THOUSAND.
Price 3s. 6d.

"An original exposition, marked by strong common sense and practical exhortation."—*Literary Churchman.*

ISAAC, JACOB, AND JOSEPH.
By *MARCUS DODS, D.D.*
SIXTH THOUSAND.
Price 3s. 6d.

"The present volume is worthy of the writer's reputation. He deals with the problems of human life and character which these biographies suggest in a candid and manly fashion."—*Spectator.*

The Sunday Afternoon Library for Young People.

Crown 8vo, elegantly bound in cloth, 3s. 6d. each; or the Four Vols., in case, 12s.

TALKING TO THE CHILDREN.

By the Rev. ALEXANDER MACLEOD, D.D.

"An exquisite work. Divine truths are here presented in simple language, illustrated by parable and anecdote at once apt and beautiful." *Evangelical Magazine.*

THE GENTLE HEART.

By the SAME AUTHOR.

"We have been fascinated with the originality and beauty of its thought, charmed with the simplicity and elegance of its language, and enriched with the store of its illustration."—*Mr. Spurgeon.*

THE CHURCHETTE.

A Year's Sermons and Parables for the Young.

By the Rev. J. REID HOWATT.

"Mr. Howatt has learned the knack of speaking to young people. Short, simple, cheery, colloquial, imaginative, impressive, the sermons yield abundant evidence that, as he says, his 'aim has been to speak to children in the sunshine.'"—*Literary World.*

"As breezy and refreshing as the breath of the ocean."—*Nonconformist.*

THE CHILDREN'S PORTION.

By the Rev. ALEXANDER MACLEOD, D.D.

"As a preacher to children, Dr. Macleod has, perhaps, no living equal. In these delightful chapters he seems to us to be at his best."—*Christian.*

"This is a collection of short sermons addressed to children. They are well adapted to strike the fancy and touch the heart of the young."—*Record.*

THE CRITICAL AND EXPOSITORY BIBLE CYCLOPÆDIA.

By the Rev. *A. R. FAUSSET, D.D.*, Canon of York, Joint Author of "The Critical and Experimental Commentary."

Illustrated by Six Hundred Woodcuts.

Cheap Edition, Unabridged. Eighth Thousand. 7s. 6d., *cloth, red edges.*

"This is a work of prodigious research, labour, and minute painstaking. The book is a rich and full storehouse of Scripture knowledge."—*Guardian.*

"I am glad to bear testimony to its accuracy and value. It accomplishes the purpose of putting the results of modern scholarship in a popular form."—*Rev. Alex. Maclaren, D.D.*

THE NEWBERRY BIBLE.

Comprising the
English-Hebrew Bible and the English-Greek Testament.

Designed to give as far as practicable the Accuracy, Precision, and Certainty of the Original Hebrew and Greek Scriptures on the page of the Authorised Version. Adapted both for the Biblical Student and for the Ordinary English Reader.

Edited by *THOMAS NEWBERRY.*

LARGE TYPE HANDY REFERENCE EDITION.

21s., 25s., 35s., *and a very superior Edition, in best Levant Yapp, kid lined, silk sewn,* 60s. *Portable Edition,* 18s., 28s., 35s.

Among the Prominent Features are the following :—

AUTHORISED VERSION arranged in Paragraphs.
Leading Words and Emphatic Pronouns in distinctive type.
Poetical Portions arranged in parallels.
Parallel passages connected and references given.
Imperfect translations emended. Original Hebrew and Greek words inserted in margin.
Divine titles distinguished and explained.
Singular, dual, and plural numbers distinguished.
Important words traced to their Hebrew and Greek roots.
Hebrew and Greek tenses marked by simple and uniform signs.
The use and force of the letter "vau" or conjunction "and" shown.
Words translated by two or more words connected by a hyphen.
The signs employed are of the simplest possible character.

WORKS BY DR. R. W. DALE, of Birmingham.

FELLOWSHIP WITH CHRIST,

And other Discourses Delivered on Special Occasions.

THIRD THOUSAND.

Crown 8vo, cloth, price 6s.

"These are certainly among the most massive, and, as a consequence, most impressive sermons of the day. Each is a sort of miniature theological treatise, but the theology is alive—as it were, heated through and through by the fires of a mighty conviction, which has become a passion to convince. . . . In these sermons there is a fine universalism; they might be addressed to any audience—academic, professional, commercial, artisan. And to hear them would be to feel that religion is a thing to be believed and obeyed."—*Speaker.*

THE LIVING CHRIST AND THE FOUR GOSPELS.

FIFTH THOUSAND.

Crown 8vo, cloth, price 6s.

"As a man of culture and eloquence he has put the case strongly and well, and it will not be surprising if his book, which is not written, he tells us, for Masters of Arts, but in the first instance for members of his own congregation, and then for all ordinary people who take an interest in such matters, should be the means of convincing many that the assumptions sometimes made about late origin of the Gospels, etc., are utterly unfounded."—*Scotsman.*

LAWS OF CHRIST FOR COMMON LIFE.

FIFTH THOUSAND.

Crown 8vo, price 6s.

"Sound sense and wholesome Christian teaching conveyed in pure, idiomatic, and forcible English."—*Scotsman.*

"A storehouse of wise precepts, a repository of loving counsels—shrewd, practical, and fully cognisant of difficulties and drawbacks; but informed by such sympathy and a sense of Christian brotherhood as should do much to make it acceptable and effective."—*Nonconformist.*

WORKS BY DR R. W. DALE (continued).

NINE LECTURES ON PREACHING.

Sixth Edition. Crown 8vo, price 6s.

"Admirable lectures, briefly written, earnest and practical."—*Literary Churchman.*

"Dr. Dale's lectures are full of practical wisdom and intense devotion."—*The Expositor.*

THE JEWISH TEMPLE AND THE CHRISTIAN CHURCH.

A Series of Discourses on the Epistle to the Hebrews.

Eighth Edition. Crown 8vo, price 6s.

"Wholesomer sermons than these it is almost impossible to conceive. Mr. Dale's preaching has always been remarkable for moral energy and fervour, but here this characteristic rises to its highest power."—*Expositor*

THE EPISTLE TO THE EPHESIANS.

Its Doctrines and Ethics.

Sixth Edition. Crown 8vo, price 7s. 6d.

"The terse and vigorous style, rising on occasion into a manly and impressive eloquence, of which Mr. Dale is known to be a master, gives lucid expression to thought that is precise, courageous, and original."—*Spectator.*

WEEK-DAY SERMONS.

Fifth Edition. Crown 8vo, price 3s. 6d.

"Dr. Dale is certainly an admirable teacher of Christian ethics. He is, perhaps, the greatest living successor of the Apostle James. In this volume he appears at his best."—*Christian.*

THE TEN COMMANDMENTS.

Sixth Edition. Crown 8vo, price 5s.

"Full of thought and vigour."—*Spectator.*

IMPRESSIONS OF AUSTRALIA.

Crown 8vo, cloth, price 5s.

"Dr. Dale's articles ... constitute one of the most sensible books about Australia. . The book is readable, and indeed excellent."—*Athenæum.*

THE NEW EVANGELICALISM AND THE OLD.

Cloth, price 1s.

"It has more in it than many an elaborate treatise; it suggests by every sentence; it is throughout succinct, pregnant, masterly."—*British Weekly.*

CPSIA information can be obtained
at www.ICGtesting.com
Printed in the USA
LVOW04s0053280716
498080LV00027B/866/P